POCKET CHEF

Juicing

igloobooks

Published in 2016
by Igloo Books Ltd
Cottage Farm
Sywell
NN6 0BJ
www.igloobooks.com

Food photography and recipe development:
© Stockfood, The Food Media Agency
Cover image © Marilyn Conway / Getty Images

HUN001 0616
2 4 6 8 10 9 7 5 3
ISBN: 978-1-78557-533-4

Cover designed by Nicholas Gage
Interiors designed by Charles Wood-Penn
Edited by Natalie Baker

Printed and manufactured in China

Contents

Fruit Burst

Strawberry and Banana Smoothie

SERVES 4

PREPARATION TIME 10 MINUTES

INGREDIENTS

2 small ripe bananas, chopped

300 g / 10 ½ oz / 2 cups strawberries, hulled
    and chopped

2 tbsp honey

225 g / 8 oz / 1 cup Greek yogurt

500 ml / 18 fl. oz / 2 cups semi-skimmed milk

METHOD

1. Combine all of the ingredients in a food processor or blender.

2. Blend on high until smooth.

3. Pour into glasses and serve.

TOP TIP

Adjust the amount of honey used to suit your tastes.

FRUIT BURST

Strawberry and Melon Juice

SERVES 4

PREPARATION TIME 15 MINUTES

INGREDIENTS

300 g / 10 ½ oz / 2 cups strawberries, hulled
    and chopped
½ small watermelon, seeded and flesh diced
250 g / 9 oz / 1 cup crushed ice
2–3 tbsp light agave nectar

METHOD

1. Combine the fruit and ice in a blender or food processor.

2. Blend until smooth; 1–2 minutes.

3. Add some of the nectar and blend until combined, then taste. Add more syrup if needed, blending again.

4. Divide between glasses and serve.

TOP TIP

Mash the fruit first in step 1 if you are having trouble blending.

Peach and Strawberry Juice

SERVES **4**

PREPARATION TIME **10 MINUTES**

INGREDIENTS

4 large, ripe peaches, peeled, pitted and sliced
450 g / 1 lb / 3 cups frozen strawberries
200 g / 7 oz / 1 cup peach yogurt
250 ml / 9 fl. oz / 1 cup water
2 large strawberries, hulled and sliced

METHOD

1. Combine all the ingredients in a blender or food processor.

2. Blend for 1–2 minutes, pausing once to stir, until combined.

3. Divide between glasses and garnish with strawberries on the rim.

TOP TIP

Canned peaches can be used in a pinch, if fresh are not available.

Raspberry and Orange Juice

SERVES 4

PREPARATION TIME 10 MINUTES

INGREDIENTS

400 g / 14 oz / 2 ⅔ cups raspberries
225 g / 8 oz / 1 cup crushed ice
2 large oranges, juiced
250 ml / 9 fl. oz / 1 cup cold water
2–3 tbsp light agave nectar

METHOD

1. Pulse together the raspberries and ice in a blender or food processor.

2. Add the orange juice, water and agave nectar to taste. Blend for 1 minute until smooth.

3. Pour into glasses and serve.

TOP TIP
Add more or less agave nectar to cater to your tastes.

Pear and Raspberry Juice

SERVES **4**

PREPARATION TIME **10 MINUTES**

INGREDIENTS

2 large Rocha pears, peeled, cored and diced
300 g / 10 ½ oz / 2 cups frozen raspberries
2 tbsp caster (superfine) sugar
400 ml / 14 fl. oz / 1 ⅔ cups water

METHOD

1. Blend the pears, raspberries and sugar in a blender or food processor until smooth and the sugar has dissolved; 2 minutes.

2. Thin the mixture with the water and blend again.

3. Pour into a jug and divide between serving glasses.

TOP TIP

To make a smoothie, add 150 g / 5 oz / ⅔ cup of Greek yogurt when blending.

Fresh Apple Juice

SERVES 4

PREPARATION TIME 20 MINUTES

INGREDIENTS

110 ml / 4 fl. oz / ½ cup water
600 g / 1 lb 5 oz / 4 cups Golden Delicious apples, cored and chopped
900 g / 2 lb / 6 cups Granny Smith apples, cored and chopped

METHOD

1. Pour the water into a food processor or blender, then add the chopped apples.

2. Blend at a low setting, increasing the speed gradually, until the mixture is puréed. Continue for 30 seconds, scraping down the sides if necessary.

3. Scrape the purée into a bowl lined with a double layer of cheesecloth.

4. Bring the edges of the cheesecloth around the purée and twist well to extract as much juice as possible. Leave the mixture to strain for 10 minutes.

5. Serve immediately or cover and chill until cold.

TOP TIP
Try different varieties of apple for a slightly different taste.

Apple and Raspberry Juice

SERVES 4

PREPARATION TIME 15 MINUTES

INGREDIENTS

150 ml / 5 fl. oz / ⅔ cup cold water
1 kg / 2 lb 4 oz / 6 ⅔ cups Braeburn apples,
   cored and grated
450 g / 1 lb / 3 cups raspberries
½ lemon, juiced
1 tbsp caster (superfine) sugar

METHOD

1. Combine the water and apples in a blender or food processor and blend until puréed, scraping down the sides if necessary.

2. Add the raspberries, lemon juice and sugar to the blender and blend for 1–2 minutes until smooth.

3. Pass the mixture through a fine sieve, collecting the juice in a bowl.

4. Serve immediately or cover and keep chilled.

TOP TIP
Thin out the juice with a little cold still or sparkling water if needed.

FRUIT BURST

Apple and Orange Juice

SERVES 4

PREPARATION TIME 10 MINUTES

INGREDIENTS

500 ml / 18 fl. oz / 2 cups orange juice
1 kg / 2 lb 4 oz / 6 ⅔ cups Braeburn apples,
    cored and grated
1 mandarin, peeled, segmented and frozen

METHOD

1. Pour the orange juice into a blender or food
   processor and add the grated apple.

2. Blend until smooth, scraping down the sides
   until the mixture is puréed and smooth.

3. Press the juice through a fine sieve and
   collect in a bowl or jug.

4. Pour into glasses and garnish with frozen
   mandarin segments.

TOP TIP

Add a cup of crushed ice when blending for a frozen version.

Fresh Orange Juice

SERVES 4

PREPARATION TIME **10 MINUTES**

INGREDIENTS

8 large Navel or Valencia oranges, peeled with pith removed

METHOD

1. Pass the oranges through a vegetable juicer, working in batches.

2. Cover and chill the juice before using.

3. Alternatively, blend the oranges in a food processor if you don't have a juicer. Pass the juice through a fine sieve before chilling and serving.

TOP TIP

Replace half of the oranges with pink grapefruit for a double citrus juice.

Orange and Mango Juice

METHOD

1. Combine the mango flesh with the lime juice, oranges and water in a food processor or blender.

2. Pulse until pulpy and then blend on high for 1 minute, until frothy.

3. Pass the mixture through a fine sieve, collecting the juice in a bowl or jug.

4. Cover and chill until cold before serving.

SERVES 4

PREPARATION TIME **10 MINUTES**

INGREDIENTS

2 large, ripe mangoes, peeled, pitted and diced
1 lime, juiced
6 large Valencia oranges, peeled with pith removed
250 ml / 9 fl. oz / 1 cup cold water

TOP TIP
Substitute the water for coconut milk for a touch of luxury.

Satsuma and Spiced Apple Juice

SERVES 4

PREPARATION TIME 1 HOUR 15 MINUTES

COOKING TIME 5 MINUTES

INGREDIENTS

7 satsumas
900 g / 2 lb / 6 cups Cox's apples, cored and diced
110 ml / 4 fl. oz / ½ cup cold water
2 x 5 cm (2 in) sticks of cinnamon
1 tbsp cloves
1 tbsp caster (superfine) sugar

METHOD

1. Peel six of the satsumas. Slice the seventh and reserve as a garnish.

2. Pulse the satsumas in a food processor or blender until broken down.

3. Add the apple and water and blend until smooth and puréed. Pass the mixture through a sieve into a large saucepan.

4. Add the spices and sugar, stir well and cook over a low heat until the sugar has dissolved.

5. Remove the saucepan from the heat and leave the spices to steep for 1 hour.

6. Chill and serve the juice with a garnish of satsuma and spices.

TOP TIP

Warming spices such as cardamom and nutmeg would also work well in this recipe.

Mixed Berry and Almond Smoothie

SERVES 4

PREPARATION TIME 15 MINUTES
PLUS OVERNIGHT SOAKING

INGREDIENTS

150 g / 5 oz / 1 ½ cups whole almonds
1 l / 1 pint 16 fl. oz / 4 cups cold water
½ tsp vanilla extract
300 g / 10 ½ oz / 2 cups frozen mixed berries
2 tbsp light agave nectar

METHOD

1. Place the almonds in a bowl and cover with the water. Leave to soak overnight until the almonds are soft.

2. The next day, drain the almonds, reserving the soaking water, and give them a quick rinse.

3. Combine the soaking liquid, almonds and vanilla extract in a food processor or blender.

4. Blend until milky and smooth. Pour the milk into a bowl lined with a double layer of cheesecloth. Strain the milk, twisting the cheesecloth to extract as much milk as possible.

5. Pour the milk back into the food processor or blender and add the frozen berries and agave nectar.

6. Blend until smooth and divide between glasses before serving.

TOP TIP

Cashews work as well as almonds in this recipe.

FRUIT BURST

Blackberry and Apple Juice

SERVES 4

PREPARATION TIME 15 MINUTES

INGREDIENTS

150 ml / 5 fl. oz / ²/₃ cup cold water
900 g / 2 lb / 6 cups Braeburn or Jazz apples,
    peeled, cored and grated
225 g / 8 oz / 1 cup crushed ice
450 g / 1 lb / 3 cups blackberries
2 tbsp caster (superfine) sugar

METHOD

1. Pour the water into a food processor or
   blender and add the apple. Blend until
   puréed, scraping down the sides from time
   to time.

2. Add the crushed ice, blackberries and sugar.
   Blend on high for 2 minutes.

3. Divide between glasses and serve.

TOP TIP

A pinch of ground cinnamon complements the other ingredients in this juice.

Cherry Juice

METHOD

1. Combine all the ingredients in a blender or food processor and blend until smooth, scraping down the sides from time to time.

2. Pass the juice through a fine sieve into a jug. Serve chilled.

SERVES 4

PREPARATION TIME 15 MINUTES

INGREDIENTS

450 g / 1 lb / 3 cups red cherries, pitted
200 g / 7 oz / 1 cup canned cherries in juice
1 tbsp lemon juice
250 ml / 9 fl. oz / 1 cup water

TOP TIP

Add a handful of baby spinach leaves to the blender for a boost of iron.

FRUIT BURST

Dragon Fruit and Watermelon Juice

SERVES **4**

PREPARATION TIME **10 MINUTES**

INGREDIENTS

2 medium dragon fruit, halved with flesh
    scooped out
½ small watermelon, peeled, seeded, and
    roughly chopped
250 g / 9 oz / 1 cup crushed ice
2 tbsp honey

METHOD

1. Place all the ingredients in a blender or food
   processor and blend on high for 1–2 minutes
   until smooth.

2. Divide between glasses and serve.

TOP TIP
Add the juice of a lime
for acidity and a dose
of vitamin C.

FRUIT BURST

Watermelon Juice

SERVES **4**

PREPARATION TIME **15 MINUTES**

INGREDIENTS

1 small watermelon
250 g / 9 oz / 1 cup crushed ice
1 tbsp lime juice
2 tbsp light agave nectar

METHOD

1. Cut the watermelon into slices, removing the seeds.

2. Cut one slice into wedges and reserve as a garnish.

3. Cube the flesh from the remaining slices and combine with the ice, lime juice and agave nectar in a blender or food processor.

4. Blend until smooth. Divide between glasses and garnish with a wedge of watermelon before serving.

TOP TIP

Add a small handful of mint leaves when blending for a pop of freshness.

FRUIT BURST

Pink Grapefruit Juice

METHOD

1. Pass the fruit through a juicer, in batches, collecting the juice.

2. Chill until cold before serving.

SERVES 4

PREPARATION TIME 15 MINUTES

INGREDIENTS

6 large pink grapefruit, peeled with pith removed
2 large Valencia oranges, peeled with
    pith removed

TOP TIP
Try topping up this juice with sparkling water for a refreshing long drink.

Passion Fruit Burst

SERVES 4

PREPARATION TIME **10 MINUTES**

INGREDIENTS

4 passion fruit, halved
1 small Cantaloupe melon, cut into slices
250 ml / 9 fl. oz / 1 cup orange juice
2 tbsp honey
250 g / 9 oz / 1 cup crushed ice

METHOD

1. Scoop out the pulp from the passion fruit halves. Pass through a sieve into a food processor or blender.

2. Dice the flesh from most of the melon slices, reserving a couple of small slices as a garnish.

3. Add the melon flesh, orange juice, honey and ice to the passion fruit juice. Blend on high for 1–2 minutes until smooth.

4. Pour into glasses and garnish with slices of melon before serving.

TOP TIP

Honeydew or Galia melon would work equally well in this juice.

Pineapple, Peach and Citrus Juice

SERVES 4

PREPARATION TIME **15 MINUTES**

INGREDIENTS

1 large pineapple, peeled, cored and diced
2 limes, juiced
4 ripe peaches, peeled, pitted and sliced
250 ml / 9 fl. oz / 1 cup cold water
250 g / 9 oz / 1 cup crushed ice

METHOD

1. Combine all the ingredients in a food processor or blender.

2. Blend on high for 2 minutes until completely smooth.

3. Divide between glasses and serve.

TOP TIP

Canned peaches can be used; drain from their syrup or juice before blending.

Kiwi and Apple Juice

SERVES 4

PREPARATION TIME 10 MINUTES

INGREDIENTS

00 g / 2 lb / 6 cups Granny Smith apples,
    cored and chopped
 kiwi fruit, peeled and chopped
50 ml / 9 fl. oz / 1 cup cold water

METHOD

1. Pass the apple and kiwi fruit through a juicer, collecting the juice.

2. Mix with the cold water, divide between glasses and serve.

TOP TIP

Substitute half the apples for 300 g / 11 oz / 2 cups of white seedless grapes.

FRUIT BURST

Apricot Smoothie

SERVES 4

PREPARATION TIME 20 MINUTES

INGREDIENTS

900 g / 2 lb / 6 cups apricots, peeled, pitted
    and chopped
75 g / 3 oz / ⅓ cup caster (superfine) sugar
225 ml / 8 fl. oz / 1 cup water
500 ml / 18 fl. oz / 2 cups semi-skimmed
    milk, cold
250 g / 9 oz / 1 cup low-fat vanilla yogurt
110 g / 4 oz / ½ cup crushed ice

METHOD

1. Combine the apricots, sugar and water in a
   large saucepan.

2. Cook over a medium heat, stirring
   occasionally, until the apricots are soft;
   8–10 minutes.

3. Purée the mixture in a blender or food
   processor and pass through a sieve into
   a bowl.

4. Pour most of the purée into a food processor
   and blend with the milk, yogurt and crushed
   ice until smooth.

5. Divide between glasses and garnish with the
   remaining apricot purée before serving.

TOP TIP

Blend in 75 g / 3 oz /
¾ cup of ground
almonds for an added
boost.

Exotic Smoothie

METHOD

1. Scoop the seeds and flesh from the passion fruit into a food processor.

2. Add the mango, lime juice, milk, ice, yogurt and honey. Blend on high for 1–2 minutes until smooth.

3. Pour into glasses and serve.

SERVES 4

PREPARATION TIME 10 MINUTES

INGREDIENTS

passion fruit, halved
mango, peeled, pitted and diced
lime, juiced
00 ml / 18 fl. oz / 2 cups semi-skimmed milk
25 g / 8 oz / 1 cup crushed ice
25 g / 8 oz / 1 cup plain yogurt
tbsp honey

TOP TIP
Substitute the milk and yogurt for coconut milk and almond yogurt for a lactose-free version.

Vegetable Fix

Carrot Juice

METHOD

1. Combine the water, grated carrot, lemon juice and ginger in a blender or food processor.

2. Blend on a low setting to start with. Add the crushed ice, then increase to high and blend for a further minute until smooth.

3. Pour into glasses and serve.

SERVES 4

PREPARATION TIME 10 MINUTES

INGREDIENTS

500 ml / 18 fl. oz / 2 cups cold water
450 g / 1 lb / 3 cups carrots, peeled and grated
1 tbsp lemon juice
½ tsp root ginger, grated
110 g / 4 oz / ½ cup crushed ice

TOP TIP
This juice should be served as soon as possible for best results.

Carrot, Coriander and Orange Juice

SERVES 4

PREPARATION TIME 15 MINUTES

INGREDIENTS

- large carrots, peeled
- Valencia oranges, halved and juiced
- 250 ml / 9 fl. oz / 1 cup cold water
- 225 g / 8 oz / 1 cup crushed ice
- tbsp lemon juice
- a small bunch of coriander (cilantro), chopped

METHOD

1. Grate most of the carrots and peel half of one into strips using a vegetable peeler.

2. Combine the grated carrot with the orange juice and water in a food processor or blender.

3. Blend on a low setting for 30 seconds. Add the ice, lemon juice and most of the coriander.

4. Blend on high for 1 minute until smooth. Pour into glasses and serve with a garnish of the prepared carrot strips and coriander.

TOP TIP

Try using mint instead of coriander for a sweet freshness in the juice.

Spinach Smoothie

METHOD

1. Blend the spinach, ice, yogurt and milk in a food processor or blender until smooth.

2. Adjust the sweetness and acidity to taste by adding a little of the agave nectar and lemon juice and blending.

3. Add more if needed, then pour into glasses and serve.

SERVES 4

PREPARATION TIME 10 MINUTES

INGREDIENTS

200 g / 7 oz / 4 cups baby spinach, washed
225 g / 8 oz / 1 cup crushed ice
225 g / 8 oz / 1 cup plain yogurt
350 ml / 12 fl. oz / 1 ½ cups almond milk
1–2 tsp light agave nectar
1–2 tsp lemon juice

TOP TIP
You may need to scrape down the sides of the blender to incorporate the spinach.

Cucumber and Avocado Smoothie

SERVES 4

PREPARATION TIME 15 MINUTES

INGREDIENTS

1 large cucumber, diced
1 ripe avocado, peeled, pitted and diced
1 kiwi fruit, peeled and diced
500 ml / 18 fl. oz / 2 cups semi-skimmed milk
150 g / 5 oz / 2/3 cup plain yogurt
1 lime, juiced
225 g / 8 oz / 1 cup crushed ice

METHOD

1. Combine the cucumber, avocado, kiwi fruit, milk, yogurt and lime juice in a blender or food processor.

2. Blend until smooth. Add the ice and blend again for a further minute.

3. Pour into glasses and serve.

TOP TIP
Add 1 tbsp of agave nectar for a sweeter version.

Kale Smoothie

METHOD

1. Combine the kale, celery, banana, apple juice, water and lemon juice in a food processor or blender.

2. Stir well and blend on high until frothy.

3. Add the ice and blend again until smooth. Pour into glasses and serve.

SERVES **4**

PREPARATION TIME **15 MINUTES**

INGREDIENTS

300 g / 10 ½ oz / 2 cups kale, chopped
2 sticks of celery, peeled and diced
½ small banana, diced
250 ml / 9 fl. oz / 1 cup apple juice
350 ml / 12 fl. oz / 1 ½ cups cold water
1 tbsp lemon juice
110 g / 4 oz / ½ cup crushed ice

TOP TIP

Cut out the centre ribs from the kale as these can be tough.

Cucumber, Spinach and Pear Smoothie

SERVES 4

PREPARATION TIME **10 MINUTES**

INGREDIENTS

1 large cucumber, peeled and diced
150 g / 5 oz / 3 cups baby spinach, washed
2 Rocha pears, peeled, cored, and diced
250 g / 9 oz / 1 cup plain yogurt
500 ml / 18 fl. oz / 2 cups almond milk
110 g / 4 oz / ½ cup crushed ice

METHOD

1. Combine the cucumber, spinach, pear, yogurt and almond milk in a food processor.

2. Blend on a low setting for 1 minute, scraping down the sides from time to time.

3. Add the ice and blend on high for a further minute.

4. Pour into glasses and serve immediately.

TOP TIP

Use coconut milk instead of almond for a richer smoothie.

Beetroot, Celery and Carrot Juice

SERVES 4

PREPARATION TIME 10 MINUTES

INGREDIENTS

300 g / 10 ½ oz / 2 cups cooked beetroot,
    roughly chopped
2 large carrots, roughly chopped
250 ml / 9 fl. oz / 1 cup apple juice, chilled
250 ml / 9 fl. oz / 1 cup cold water

METHOD

1. Pass the beetroot and carrots though a vegetable juicer, collecting the juice.

2. Stir the juice with the apple juice and water and divide between glasses before serving.

TOP TIP

If using ready-cooked beetroot, make sure they are preserved in juice, not vinegar.

Beetroot Smoothie

METHOD

1. Combine all the ingredients in a food processor or blender.

2. Blend on high until smooth, then divide between glasses and serve.

SERVES 4

PREPARATION TIME 10 MINUTES

INGREDIENTS

150 g / 9 oz / 1 cup crushed ice
500 g / 1 lb / 3 cups cooked beetroot, chopped
125 g / 4 ½ oz / ½ cup plain yogurt
125 ml / 4 ½ fl. oz / ½ cup apple juice

TOP TIP

Try replacing the yogurt with light coconut milk for a luxurious smoothie.

Spicy Tomato Juice

SERVES 4

PREPARATION TIME 15 MINUTES

INGREDIENTS

2 sticks of celery
450 g / 1 lb / 3 cups cherry tomatoes, chopped
250 ml / 9 fl. oz / 1 cup cold water
1 tbsp caster (superfine) sugar
a dash of Worcestershire sauce
1 tsp hot sauce
1 lemon, halved
1 lime, cut into wedges
flaked sea salt and freshly ground black pepper

METHOD

1. Remove the leafy tops from the celery and reserve as a garnish. Peel and chop the sticks.

2. Combine them with the tomatoes, water, sugar, Worcestershire sauce, hot sauce and some seasoning in a food processor or blender.

3. Blend on high until smooth; 1–2 minutes. Pass the juice through a sieve into a jug and squeeze in a little lemon juice, stirring well.

4. Rub the rims of four serving glasses with the lemon halves. Dip the rims in flaked sea salt and fill with the tomato juice.

5. Season with black pepper and garnish with lime wedges and celery leaves before serving.

TOP TIP
Add more or less hot sauce to cater to your tastes.

Red Cabbage and Apple Juice

SERVES 4

PREPARATION TIME 10 MINUTES

INGREDIENTS

red cabbage, shredded
large Cox's apples, peeled, cored and diced
tbsp lemon juice
00 ml / 18 fl. oz / 2 cups cold water
25 g / 4 ½ oz / ½ cup crushed ice

METHOD

1. Pass the cabbage and apple through a vegetable juicer; collect the juice.

2. Pour the juice into a blender or food processor and add the lemon juice, water, and crushed ice.

3. Blend until frothy before pouring into serving glasses.

TOP TIP

The red cabbage can be substituted for white cabbage for a lighter juice.

Pepper and Carrot Juice

METHOD

1. Combine the peppers, carrots, grapes and water in a food processor or blender.

2. Blend on high until smooth, then add the crushed ice.

3. Blend again for another minute until smoot and frothy.

4. Pour into glasses and serve immediately.

SERVES 4

PREPARATION TIME 15 MINUTES

INGREDIENTS

2 red peppers, seeded and diced
4 large carrots, peeled and grated
150 g / 5 oz / 1 cup seedless red grapes
250 ml / 9 fl. oz / 1 cup cold water
250 g / 9 oz / 1 cup crushed ice

TOP TIP

Using yellow or green peppers works just as well in this juice.

Broccoli and Greens Juice

SERVES 4

PREPARATION TIME 15 MINUTES

INGREDIENTS

1 small head of broccoli, prepared into florets
2 heads of pak choi, leaves separated
150 g / 5 oz / 1 cup seedless white grapes
1 ripe avocado, peeled, pitted and diced
2 tbsp lemon juice
225 g / 8 oz / 1 cup crushed ice

METHOD

1. Pass the broccoli and pak choi through a vegetable juicer; collect the juice.

2. Combine the juice with the grapes, avocado, lemon juice and crushed ice in a food processor or blender.

3. Blend on high for 1–2 minutes until smooth.

4. Pour into glasses and serve.

TOP TIP
Try adding a cup of plain yogurt for a smoothie version.

Smoothie Bar

Strawberry Smoothie

SERVES **4**

PREPARATION TIME **10 MINUTES**

INGREDIENTS

450 g / 1 lb / 3 cups strawberries, hulled
   and sliced
500 ml / 18 fl. oz / 2 cups semi-skimmed milk
225 g / 8 oz / 1 cup plain yogurt
110 g / 4 oz / ½ cup crushed ice
1 lemon, halved
55 g / 2 oz / ¼ cup caster (superfine) sugar

METHOD

1. Set aside four slices of strawberry. Combine the remaining strawberries in a food processor or blender with the milk and yogurt.

2. Blend on high for 2 minutes. Add the ice and blend for a further minute until smoot

3. Rub the rims of four serving glasses with lemon juice. Dip in caster sugar and fill wi the strawberry smoothie.

4. Garnish with a slice of strawberry on the r before serving.

TOP TIP

Add 1–2 tbsp of honey when blending to make this smoothie a little sweeter.

Strawberry and Kiwi Smoothie

ERVES 4

REPARATION TIME 10 MINUTES

INGREDIENTS

50 g / 1 lb / 3 cups strawberries, hulled and
    chopped, plus 4 small strawberries
    to decorate
kiwi fruit, peeled and diced
25 ml / 8 fl. oz / 1 cup orange juice,
    freshly squeezed
50 ml / 9 fl. oz / 1 cup cold water
5 g / 4 ½ oz / ½ cup crushed ice

METHOD

1. Combine the strawberries, kiwi fruit and
   orange juice in a food processor or blender.

2. Blend on high until smooth.

3. Add the water and ice and blend again
   until smooth.

4. Pour into glasses and serve garnished with
   a strawberry.

TOP TIP

Add 1 tbsp of agave
nectar when blending
for some added
sweetness.

Strawberry and Redcurrant Smoothie

METHOD

1. Combine the fruit, honey, yogurt and milk in a food processor or blender.
2. Blend on high for 1 minute, until smooth.
3. Add the crushed ice and blend again for a further minute.
4. Pour into glasses and serve.

SERVES **4**

PREPARATION TIME **10 MINUTES**

INGREDIENTS

300 g / 10 ½ oz / 2 cups strawberries, hulled and diced
225 g / 8 oz / 1 ½ cups redcurrants
2 tbsp honey
250 g / 9 oz / 1 cup plain yogurt
500 ml / 18 fl. oz / 2 cups vanilla almond milk
125 g / 4 ½ oz / ½ cup crushed ice

TOP TIP
Scrape down the sides of the blender before adding the ice.

Blackberry and Raspberry Smoothie

METHOD

1. Combine the raspberries, blackberries, yogurt, milk and agave nectar in a food processor or blender.

2. Blend until smooth. Add the crushed ice and blend again until smooth.

3. Pour into glasses and serve.

SERVES 4

PREPARATION TIME 5 MINUTES

INGREDIENTS

300 g / 10 ½ oz / 2 cups frozen raspberries

200 g / 7 oz / 1 ⅓ cups blackberries

150 g / 5 oz / ⅔ cup vanilla yogurt

250 ml / 9 fl. oz / 1 cup semi-skimmed milk

1 tbsp light agave nectar

250 g / 9 oz / 1 cup crushed ice

TOP TIP

Add a handful of frozen blueberries for a three-berry smoothie.

Raspberry Cheesecake Smoothie

SERVES 4

PREPARATION TIME 10 MINUTES

INGREDIENTS

300 g / 10 ½ oz / 2 cups frozen raspberries
2 tbsp raspberry jam (jelly)
225 g / 8 oz / 1 cup cream cheese
2 digestive biscuits, crushed
1 tbsp rolled oats
750 ml / 1 pint 6 fl. oz / 3 cups semi-skimmed
    milk
a handful of raspberries
a handful of golden raspberries

METHOD

1. Combine the frozen raspberries, raspberr
   jam, cream cheese, digestive biscuits, roll
   oats and milk in a food processor or blende

2. Blend on high for 2 minutes, scraping dow
   the sides after 1 minute.

3. Pour into glasses and serve with skewers c
   the raspberries.

TOP TIP

Use low-fat cream cheese or Greek yogurt for a healthier version.

Beetroot and Raspberry Smoothie

SERVES 4

PREPARATION TIME 5 MINUTES

INGREDIENTS

300 g / 10 ½ oz / 2 cups cooked beetroot in juice
300 g / 10 ½ oz / 2 cups raspberries
250 g / 9 oz / 1 cup plain yogurt
1 tbsp light agave nectar
225 g / 8 oz / 1 cup crushed ice

METHOD

1. Combine the beetroot and their juice with the raspberries, yogurt and agave nectar in a food processor or blender.

2. Blend on high for 1 minute.

3. Add the crushed ice and blend again for another minute.

4. Pour into glasses and serve.

TOP TIP

Replace the yogurt with water for a thinner, lactose-free version.

Berry Smoothie with Pomegranate

SERVES 4

PREPARATION TIME 10 MINUTES

INGREDIENTS

1 pomegranate, halved
150 g / 5 oz / 1 cup frozen raspberries
150 g / 5 oz / 1 cup frozen strawberries
500 ml / 18 fl. oz / 2 cups semi-skimmed milk
2 tbsp honey
125 g / 4 ½ oz / ½ cup crushed ice

METHOD

1. Tap the back of the pomegranate with a wooden spoon to release the seeds. Add three-quarters of them to a food processor or blender along with the frozen fruit and milk.

2. Blend on high for 1 minute and then add the honey and crushed ice. Blend again until incorporated.

3. Pour into glasses or serving bottles and garnish with the remaining pomegranate seeds.

TOP TIP

Replace the honey with strawberry jam (jelly).

Blueberry and Lavender Smoothie

ERVES **4**

REPARATION TIME **5 MINUTES**

NGREDIENTS

50 g / 1 lb / 3 cups frozen blueberries
25 g / 8 oz / 1 cup vanilla ice cream
50 ml / 12 fl. oz / 1 ½ cups semi-skimmed milk
25 g / 4 ½ oz / ½ cup crushed ice
few drops of lavender essence
few sprigs of lavender

METHOD

1. Combine the blueberries with the ice cream and milk in a food processor or blender.

2. Blend on high for 1 minute.

3. Scrape down the sides and add the ice and a few drops of lavender essence. Blend again and taste, adding more lavender essence if needed.

4. Pour and scrape into glasses and serve with a garnish of lavender.

TOP TIP
Use fresh blueberries for a thinner consistency.

Blueberry and Goji Berry Smoothie

SERVES 4

PREPARATION TIME 20 MINUTES

INGREDIENTS

55 g / 2 oz / 1/3 cup dried goji berries
300 g / 10 ½ oz / 2 cups frozen blueberries
1 large banana, chopped
1 tbsp light agave nectar
250 ml / 9 fl. oz / 1 cup almond milk

METHOD

1. Soak the goji berries in 150 ml / ¼ oz / 2/3 cup of hot water, leaving the water to cool.

2. Combine the berries and soaking liquid in a food processor or blender with the blueberries, banana, agave nectar and milk.

3. Blend on high for 1–2 minutes until smooth.

4. Pour into glasses and serve.

TOP TIP
Omit the agave nectar for a lower sugar version.

Banana and Goji Berry Smoothie

SERVES 4

PREPARATION TIME 20 MINUTES

INGREDIENTS

90 g / 5 oz / 1 cup dried goji berries

750 ml / 1 pint 6 fl. oz / 3 cups semi-skimmed milk

2 tbsp light agave nectar

2 large, ripe bananas, chopped

100 g / 4 oz / ½ cup crushed ice

METHOD

1. Set aside 1 tbsp of the goji berries.

2. Combine the rest of the berries with the milk in a food processor or blender and soak for 10 minutes.

3. Add the agave nectar and banana, then blend on high for 2 minutes.

4. Add the crushed ice and blend again until frothy. Pour into glasses and serve with a garnish of the remaining goji berries.

TOP TIP
Add 2 tbsp of vanilla yogurt when blending for a thicker smoothie.

Banana and Pineapple Smoothie

SERVES 4

PREPARATION TIME 10 MINUTES

INGREDIENTS

4 medium ripe bananas, chopped
1 small pineapple, peeled, cored and diced
250 ml / 9 fl. oz / 1 cup semi-skimmed milk
125 g / 4 ½ oz / ½ cup vanilla yogurt
250 g / 9 oz / 1 cup crushed ice

METHOD

1. Combine the banana, pineapple, milk and yogurt in a food processor or blender.

2. Blend on high for 2 minutes, scraping down the sides occasionally, until completely smooth.

3. Add the crushed ice and blend again for 1 minute.

4. Pour into glasses and serve.

TOP TIP
Add 1 tbsp of agave nectar or honey for a sweeter smoothie.

Pineapple and Coconut Smoothie

METHOD

1. Combine the pineapple, lime juice, coconut milk and vanilla extract in a food processor or blender.

2. Blend on high until smooth. Add the crushed ice and blend again for a further minute.

3. Pour into glasses and serve immediately.

SERVES 4

PREPARATION TIME 10 MINUTES

INGREDIENTS

small pineapple, peeled, cored and diced

lime, juiced

0 ml / 14 fl. oz / 1 2/3 cups light coconut milk, chilled

tsp vanilla extract

5 g / 8 oz / 1 cup crushed ice

TOP TIP

For a thick smoothie, use regular coconut milk and add 2 tbsp of Greek yogurt.

Papaya and Peach Smoothie

SERVES **4**

PREPARATION TIME **15 MINUTES**

INGREDIENTS

2 tbsp rolled oats
500 ml / 18 fl. oz / 2 cups semi-skimmed milk
4 peaches, pitted, skinned and diced
1 small papaya, peeled, seeded and diced
1 lime, juiced
1 small banana, chopped
1 tbsp honey
225 g / 8 oz / 1 cup crushed ice

METHOD

1. Combine the oats and milk in a blender. Leave to soak for 5 minutes.

2. Add the peaches, papaya, lime juice, banana and honey. Blend on high for 2 minutes until smooth.

3. Add the ice and blend again for a further minute.

4. Pour into glasses and serve.

TOP TIP
Use canned peaches or papaya if either is not available to buy fresh.

Mango, Passion Fruit and Coconut Smoothie

SERVES 4

PREPARATION TIME 20 MINUTES

INGREDIENTS

passion fruit, halved

lime

mango, peeled, pitted and diced

0 ml / 14 fl. oz / 1 ²/₃ cups coconut milk, chilled

0 ml / 9 fl. oz / 1 cup cold water

bsp light agave nectar

5 g / 8 oz / 1 cup crushed ice

g / 3 oz / 1 cup desiccated coconut

METHOD

1. Scoop the pulp and seeds from the passion fruit halves into a sieve set over a bowl. Pass the pulp and flesh through the sieve, collecting the purée in the bowl.

2. Finely zest the lime, then cut it in half, cutting one half into wedges. Squeeze the other half into the passion fruit purée and stir in the grated zest.

3. Scrape the passion fruit and lime juice purée into a food processor or blender and add the mango, coconut milk, water and agave nectar.

4. Blend on high for 2 minutes. Stir well, add the ice and blend for a further minute.

5. Rub the rims of four serving glasses with the lime wedges. Dip in a shallow plate of the desiccated coconut to coat the rims.

6. Fill with the smoothie and serve immediately.

TOP TIP
For a thicker smoothie, add a dollop of vanilla ice cream before blending.

Lychee, Cherry and Apple Smoothie

SERVES **4**

PREPARATION TIME **10 MINUTES**

INGREDIENTS

250 ml / 9 fl. oz / 1 cup cherry juice
250 ml / 9 fl. oz / 1 cup apple juice
200 g / 7 oz / 1 cup canned lychees in syrup
225 g / 8 oz / 1 cup Greek yogurt
110 g / 4 oz / ½ cup crushed ice

METHOD

1. Combine the cherry juice, apple juice, lychees and 2 tbsp of their syrup in a food processor or blender.

2. Blend on high for 1 minute. Add a generous dollop of the Greek yogurt as well as the crushed ice.

3. Blend for a further minute until smooth.

4. Pour into glasses and serve with dollops of the remaining yogurt.

TOP TIP

Try to use pressed, cloudy apple juice for best results.

Apricot and Almond Smoothie

METHOD

1. Combine the ground almonds and milk in a food processor or blender. Leave to soak for 5 minutes.

2. Add the apricots and their juice as well as the crushed ice. Blend on high for 2 minutes until smooth.

3. Pour into glasses, garnish with flaked almonds, and serve with the biscuits on the side.

SERVES 4

PREPARATION TIME 10 MINUTES

INGREDIENTS

g / 2 oz / ½ cup ground almonds
0 ml / 18 fl. oz / 2 cups semi-skimmed milk
0 g / 14 oz / 2 cups canned apricots in juice
0 g / 4 oz / ½ cup crushed ice
g / 2 oz / ½ cup flaked (slivered) almonds
nger biscuits, to serve

TOP TIP

Add a generous pinch of ground cinnamon before blending for a hint of warm spice.

Pumpkin Spice Smoothie

SERVES **4**

PREPARATION TIME **10 MINUTES**

INGREDIENTS

400 g / 14 oz / 2 cups canned pumpkin purée
2 tbsp honey
750 ml / 1 pint 6 fl. oz / 3 cups semi-skimmed
   milk
1 tsp ground cinnamon
a pinch of ground nutmeg
a pinch of ground ginger
225 g / 8 oz / 1 cup crushed ice
225 ml / 8 fl. oz / 1 cup double (heavy) cream
2 tbsp icing (confectioners') sugar

METHOD

1. Combine the pumpkin purée, honey and milk with a pinch of ground cinnamon, nutmeg and ginger in a food processor or blender.

2. Blend on high for 1 minute, add the crushed ice and blend again until completely smooth.

3. In a mixing bowl, whip the cream with the icing sugar until softly peaked.

4. Pour the smoothie into glasses and top with mounds of the whipped cream. Garnish with a dusting of the remaining ground cinnamon.

TOP TIP
Serve with a scoop of vanilla ice cream on top for a quick dessert.

Rocket and Cucumber Smoothie

SERVES 4

PREPARATION TIME 10 MINUTES

INGREDIENTS

cucumber
100 g / 3 ½ oz / 2 cups rocket (arugula), washed
lemon, juiced
225 g / 8 oz / 1 cup plain yogurt
tbsp caster (superfine) sugar
225 g / 8 oz / 1 cup crushed ice

METHOD

1. Carefully slice four thin strips from the cucumber and thread them onto toothpicks, then dice the remaining cucumber.

2. Combine the diced cucumber with the rocket, lemon juice, yogurt and sugar in a food processor or blender.

3. Blend on high for 2 minutes. Scrape down the sides, stir well and add the crushed ice.

4. Blend again for a further minute.

5. Pour into glasses and serve with a garnish of the cucumber slices on toothpicks.

TOP TIP

Try replacing the yogurt with the flesh of one ripe avocado for a power smoothie.

Beetroot and Grapefruit Smoothie

SERVES **4**

PREPARATION TIME **10 MINUTES**

INGREDIENTS

2 white grapefruit, peeled and segmented
450 g / 1 lb / 3 cups cooked beetroot in juice
1 small banana, chopped
250 ml / 9 fl. oz / 1 cup orange juice
110 g / 4 oz / ½ cup crushed ice
a small bunch of mint, leaves picked

METHOD

1. Combine the grapefruit segments, beetroot and juice, banana and orange juice in a food processor or blender.

2. Blend on high for 2 minutes. Stir in the crushed ice and 1 tbsp of mint leaves, blending again for a further minute.

3. Pour into glasses and garnish with the remaining mint leaves before serving.

TOP TIP
Try different combinations of white, red and pink grapefruit.

Superfood Sensations

Blueberry and Hemp Seed Smoothie

SERVES 4

PREPARATION TIME 5 MINUTES

INGREDIENTS

350 g / 12 oz / 3 cups frozen blueberries
250 g / 9 oz / 1 cup Greek yogurt
250 ml / 9 fl. oz / 1 cup almond milk
2 tbsp honey
2 tbsp hemp seeds
150 g / 5 oz / ²/₃ cup crushed ice

METHOD

1. Combine the blueberries, yogurt, milk, honey and most of the hemp seeds in a food processor or blender.

2. Blend on high for 2 minutes. Scrape down the sides, add the crushed ice and blend again until smooth.

3. Pour into glasses and garnish with the remaining hemp seeds.

TOP TIP
Substitute the hemp seeds for chia seeds.

Blueberry, Kiwi and Grape Smoothie

SERVES **4**

REPARATION TIME **10 MINUTES**

INGREDIENTS

 kiwi fruit
50 g / 12 oz / 3 cups frozen blueberries
00 g / 10 ½ oz / 2 cups black seedless grapes
50 ml / 9 fl. oz / 1 cup cold sparkling water

METHOD

1. Slice one kiwi fruit into slices and set to one side. Peel and chop the remaining kiwi fruit.

2. Combine the chopped kiwi fruit with the blueberries, grapes and sparkling water in a food processor or blender.

3. Blend on high for 2–3 minutes until smooth.

4. Pour into glasses and serve with a slice of kiwi fruit on the rim.

TOP TIP

Add 150 g / 5 oz / ²/₃ cup of crushed ice if using fresh blueberries.

Cherry and Apple Smoothie

SERVES 4

PREPARATION TIME 10 MINUTES

INGREDIENTS

450 g / 1 lb / 3 cups red cherries, pitted
250 ml / 9 fl. oz / 1 cup apple juice
250 ml / 9 fl. oz / 1 cup raspberry cocktail juice
1 tbsp light agave nectar
225 g / 8 oz / 1 cup crushed ice
1 tbsp desiccated coconut

METHOD

1. Combine all but four of the cherries in a food processor or blender.

2. Add the apple juice, raspberry cocktail juice, agave nectar and crushed ice.

3. Blend on high for 2 minutes until smooth.

4. Pour into glasses and garnish with a cherry and some desiccated coconut.

TOP TIP

Frozen cherries can be used instead of fresh; substitute the ice with chilled water.

Cherry, Celery and Chilli Juice

SERVES 4

PREPARATION TIME 15 MINUTES

INGREDIENTS

sticks of celery
0 ml / 9 fl. oz / 1 cup cherry juice
0 ml / 9 fl. oz / 1 cup tomato juice
0 ml / 9 fl. oz / 1 cup cold water
ime, juiced
dash of hot sauce
0 g / 1 lb 2 oz / 2 cups ice cubes
lt and freshly ground black pepper

METHOD

1. Pass four of the celery sticks through a juicer, collecting the juice.

2. Combine the celery juice with the cherry juice, tomato juice, water, lime juice, hot sauce and a little seasoning in a food processor or blender.

3. Pulse a few times to combine.

4. Pour into glasses filled with ice cubes and garnish with celery sticks and a little more seasoning.

TOP TIP

The hot sauce can be omitted for a less spicy version.

Kiwi and Spinach Juice

METHOD

1. Pass the celery, grapes, spinach and kiwi fruit through a juicer, collecting the juice.

2. Stir with the cold water and divide between glasses.

SERVES 4

PREPARATION TIME 10 MINUTES

INGREDIENTS

4 sticks of celery, peeled
300 g / 10 ½ oz / 2 cups white seedless grapes
300 g / 10 ½ oz / 6 cups baby spinach
4 kiwi fruit, peeled and sliced
250 ml / 9 fl. oz / 1 cup cold water

TOP TIP

Blend in 150 g / 5 oz / ²/₃ cup of plain yogurt to make a smoothie.

Avocado, Pineapple and Citrus Smoothie

SERVES 4

PREPARATION TIME 5 MINUTES

INGREDIENTS

small pineapple, peeled, cored and diced
ripe avocado, peeled, pitted and diced
0 ml / 9 fl. oz / 1 cup light coconut milk
lime, juiced
tsp vanilla extract
5 g / 8 oz / 1 cup crushed ice
sticks of celery

METHOD

1. Combine the pineapple, avocado, coconut milk, lime juice and vanilla extract in a food processor or blender.

2. Blend on high for 2 minutes until smooth. Add the crushed ice and blend again for a further minute.

3. Pour into glasses and garnish with a stick of celery before serving.

TOP TIP

Try adding a handful of baby kale for a vitamin K boost.

Kiwi and Citrus Juice

METHOD

1. Combine the pineapple juice, kiwi fruit, lime and lemon juices in a food processor or blender.

2. Blend on high for 2 minutes, add the crushed ice, then blend for a further minute until smooth.

3. Pour into glasses and serve.

SERVES **4**

PREPARATION TIME **10 MINUTES**

INGREDIENTS

500 ml / 18 fl. oz / 2 cups pineapple juice
4 kiwi fruit, peeled and sliced
1 lime, juiced
1 lemon, juiced
225 g / 8 oz / 1 cup crushed ice

TOP TIP
Add 1 tbsp of honey to
sweeten the juice
if needed.

Orange and Papaya Juice

METHOD

1. Juice six and a half of the oranges into a food processor or blender. Slice the remaining half and reserve as a garnish.

2. Add the papaya and water, stir well, then blend on high for 2 minutes until smooth.

3. Pour into glasses filled with ice cubes. Garnish with orange slices before serving.

SERVES 4

PREPARATION TIME 10 MINUTES

INGREDIENTS

Valencia oranges, halved
papaya, peeled, seeded and cubed
00 ml / 18 fl. oz / 2 cups cold water
50 g / 9 oz / 1 cup ice cubes

TOP TIP
Strain the juice through a sieve for a smoother texture.

Mango Smoothie

SERVES 4

PREPARATION TIME 10 MINUTES

INGREDIENTS

2 large mangoes, peeled, pitted and diced
500 ml / 18 fl. oz / 2 cups plain yogurt
250 ml / 9 fl. oz / 1 cup semi-skimmed milk
1 tbsp honey
1 lime, juiced
a pinch of salt

METHOD

1. Combine the mango flesh with the yogurt, milk, honey, lime juice and salt in a food processor or blender.

2. Blend on high for 2 minutes until completel smooth.

3. Pour into glasses and serve.

TOP TIP
Top this smoothie with a little crushed cardamom for an aromatic twist.

Cantaloupe Juice

SERVES 4

PREPARATION TIME **10 MINUTES**

INGREDIENTS

large Cantaloupe melon
lime, juiced
50 ml / 9 fl. oz / 1 cup cold water
0 g / 4 oz / ½ cup crushed ice

METHOD

1. Cut the melon into thin slices and discard the seeds. Set aside four slices as a garnish and then dice the flesh of the remaining slices.

2. Blend the diced flesh with the lime juice, water and ice in a food processor or blender until smooth and frothy.

3. Pour into glasses and garnish with a slice of melon before serving.

TOP TIP

Try blending a large handful of white seedless grapes into this juice.

Lemon and Lime Juice

SERVES **4**

PREPARATION TIME **20 MINUTES**

COOKING TIME **10 MINUTES**

INGREDIENTS

6 lemons
6 limes
110 g / 4 oz / ½ cup caster (superfine) sugar
1 l / 1 pint 16 fl. oz / 4 cups water
500 g / 1 lb 2 oz / 2 cups ice cubes

METHOD

1. Juice five of the lemons and five of the limes into a saucepan and add the sugar and 250 ml / 9 fl. oz / 1 cup of the water. Cut the remaining lemon and lime into slices and set to one side.

2. Cook the citrus juice and sugar mixture over a medium heat and stir occasionally until the sugar has dissolved. Remove from the heat and leave to cool.

3. Stir in the remaining water and the ice cubes. Pour into glasses and serve with a garnish of lemon and lime slices.

TOP TIP
You can substitute the lemons and/or limes for oranges or grapefruits.

Blackberry, Apple and Cucumber Juice

METHOD

1. Combine the blackberries, apple juice, cucumber, lime juice and ice in a food processor or blender.

2. Blend on high for 2 minutes until smooth.

3. Pour into glasses and serve.

SERVES 4

PREPARATION TIME 5 MINUTES

INGREDIENTS

0 g / 12 oz / 3 cups blackberries
0 ml / 18 fl. oz / 2 cups apple juice
Large cucumber, peeled and sliced
lime, juiced
0 g / 4 oz / ½ cup crushed ice

TOP TIP
Soak a handful of rolled oats in the juice before blending for a fuller texture.

143

Gingery Beet and Apple Juice

METHOD

1. Pass the apples, beetroot and ginger through a juicer, collecting the juice.

2. Stir with the agave nectar and ice cubes until chilled.

3. Pour into glasses and serve.

SERVES 4

PREPARATION TIME **10 MINUTES**

INGREDIENTS

4 large Cox's apples, cored and diced
450 g / 1 lb / 3 cups beetroot in juice
5 cm (2 in) piece of root ginger, peeled
1 tbsp light agave nectar
250 g / 9 oz / 1 cup ice cubes

TOP TIP
For an added spicy kick, add a pinch of Cayenne pepper when stirring the juice.

Carrot and Pear Juice

ERVES 4

REPARATION TIME 10 MINUTES

INGREDIENTS

Rocha pears, peeled, cored and diced
ipe apricots, peeled, pitted and diced
arge carrots, peeled and grated
lemon, juiced
0 ml / 9 fl. oz / 1 cup cold water

METHOD

1. Combine the pears, apricots, carrots, lemon juice and water in a food processor or blender.

2. Blend on high for 2 minutes until smooth and frothy.

3. Pour into glasses and serve immediately for best results.

TOP TIP

For a sweeter juice, add 1 tbsp of honey before blending.

Tomato Super Juice

METHOD

1. Combine the tomatoes, ice, lemon juice and sugar in a food processor or blender.

2. Blend on high until smooth. Add a pinch of salt and blend again for a further minute.

3. Pour into glasses and serve.

SERVES **4**

PREPARATION TIME **10 MINUTES**

INGREDIENTS

600 g / 1 lb 5 oz / 4 cups cherry tomatoes, halved
110 g / 4 oz / ½ cup crushed ice
½ lemon, juiced
1 tbsp caster (superfine) sugar
a pinch of salt

TOP TIP

Try serving this juice with a dollop of Greek yogurt on top for a creamy addition.

Wheatgrass Juice

METHOD

1. Combine the wheatgrass, water and lemon juice in a food processor or blender.

2. Blend on high for 2 minutes.

3. Pour through a fine sieve into a bowl, pressing the pulp against the sieve with a spatula to extract as much of the juice as possible.

4. Pour the juice into glasses and serve.

SERVES 4

PREPARATION TIME 10 MINUTES

INGREDIENTS

150 g / 5 oz / ²/₃ cup wheatgrass, washed and chopped
750 ml / 1 pint 6 fl. oz / 3 cups cold water
1 tbsp lemon juice

TOP TIP

Add 2 tbsp of agave nectar before blending to make a sweeter juice.

Kale and Spinach Juice

METHOD

1. Blend together the kale, spinach, lemon juice and water in a food processor or blender until smooth.

2. Scrape down the sides and add the ice. Blend again for a further minute.

3. Pour into glasses and serve.

SERVES 4

PREPARATION TIME 10 MINUTES

INGREDIENTS

150 g / 5 oz / 3 cups baby kale
150 g / 5 oz / 3 cups baby spinach
1 lemon, juiced
250 ml / 9 fl. oz / 1 cup cold water
110 g / 4 oz / ½ cup crushed ice

TOP TIP
Add the flesh of a ripe avocado for a thicker, more luxurious drink.

Chocolate Superfood Smoothie

SERVES 4

PREPARATION TIME 20 MINUTES

INGREDIENTS

100 g / 3 ½ oz / ⅔ cup rolled oats

tbsp cocoa powder

00 ml / 14 fl. oz / 1 ⅔ cups chilled coconut milk

00 ml / 18 fl. oz / 2 cups almond milk

tbsp almond butter

tbsp light agave nectar

10 g / 4 oz / ½ cup crushed ice

tbsp dark chocolate, grated

METHOD

1. Combine most of the oats with the cocoa powder as well as the coconut and almond milk in a food processor or blender. Leave to soak for at least 10 minutes.

2. Add the almond butter and agave nectar. Blend on high for 2 minutes.

3. Add the crushed ice and blend for a further minute until smooth.

4. Pour into glasses and serve with a garnish of the remaining oats and grated chocolate.

TOP TIP

Leave the oats and cocoa powder to soak for as long as you can.

Health Boost

Health Defender

SERVES **4**

PREPARATION TIME **10 MINUTES**

INGREDIENTS

5 Rocha pears
2 Granny Smith apples, cored and grated
250 ml / 9 fl. oz / 1 cup pressed apple juice
250 ml / 9 fl. oz / 1 cup water
225 g / 8 oz / 1 cup crushed ice

METHOD

1. Core and dice four of the pears. Cut the remaining pear into long slices as a garnish.

2. Combine the diced pear, grated apple, apple juice and water in a food processor or blender.

3. Blend on high until smooth. Add the crushed ice and blend again for a further minute.

4. Pour into glasses and serve with the pear slices as a garnish.

TOP TIP
Add a large dollop of Greek yogurt before blending to make a smoothie.

Fruit Elixir

METHOD

1. Tap the back of the pomegranate halves with a wooden spoon to release the seeds.

2. Combine the seeds with the mixed berries, milk and agave nectar in a food processor or blender.

3. Blend until smooth, pour into glasses, and serve.

RVES 4

EPARATION TIME **10 MINUTES**

GREDIENTS

omegranate, halved
0 g / 1 lb / 4 cups frozen mixed berries
0 ml / 18 fl. oz / 2 cups semi-skimmed milk
bsp light agave nectar

TOP TIP

If using fresh berries, add 250 g / 9 oz / 1 cup of crushed ice to the blender.

Good For You

METHOD

1. Pass the beets and carrots through a vegetable juicer, collecting the juice.

2. Pour into a jug and stir with the water and ice cubes until chilled.

3. Pour into glasses and serve with a garnish of the olives on toothpicks.

SERVES **4**

PREPARATION TIME **10 MINUTES**

INGREDIENTS

450 g / 1 lb / 3 cups cooked beetroot in juice
600 g / 1 lb 5 oz / 4 cups carrots, peeled
250 ml / 9 fl. oz / 1 cup cold water
250 g / 9 oz / 1 cup ice cubes
8 pitted green olives

TOP TIP

Pass a thumb-sized piece of ginger through the juicer for a spicy kick.

Hangover Cure

METHOD

1. Combine the watermelon, lemon juice, water, agave nectar and most of the parsley in a food processor or blender.

2. Blend until smooth. Add the crushed ice and blend for a further minute until frothy.

3. Pour into glasses and garnish with the remaining parsley.

SERVES 4

PREPARATION TIME 10 MINUTES

INGREDIENTS

½ small watermelon, diced
1 lemon, juiced
250 ml / 9 fl. oz / 1 cup cold water
1 tbsp light agave nectar
1 small bunch of flat-leaf parsley
110 g / 4 oz / ½ cup crushed ice

TOP TIP

Experiment with different herbs such as coriander (cilantro) or mint.

HEALTH BOOST

Clear Your Head

METHOD

1. Combine the cucumber, apple juice and water in a food processor or blender.

2. Blend until smooth. Add the crushed ice and blend again for a further minute.

3. Pour into glasses and serve.

SERVES 4

PREPARATION TIME 10 MINUTES

INGREDIENTS

1 large cucumber, sliced
500 ml / 18 fl. oz / 2 cups pressed apple juice
250 ml / 9 fl. oz / 1 cup water
110 g / 4 oz / ½ cup crushed ice

TOP TIP
Add a small handful of tarragon to the mixture before blending.

Berry Boost

SERVES 4

PREPARATION TIME 5 MINUTES

INGREDIENTS

250 g / 9 oz / 2 cups raspberries
125 g / 4 ½ oz / 1 cup blueberries
250 g / 9 oz / 1 ²/₃ cups strawberries,
    hulled and chopped
150 g / 5 oz / ²/₃ cup plain yogurt
150 ml / 5 fl. oz / ²/₃ cup almond milk
1 tbsp light agave nectar
150 g / 5 oz / ²/₃ cup crushed ice
4 sprigs of mint, to garnish

METHOD

1. Combine the berries with the yogurt, milk and agave nectar in a food processor or blender.

2. Blend on high until smooth. Add the crushed ice and blend again for a further minute.

3. Pour into glasses and garnish with a sprig of mint before serving.

TOP TIP
Substitute the almond milk with coconut milk for a tropical twist.

Super Juice

METHOD

1. Combine the carrot, water, peaches, nectarines and lime juice in a food processor or blender.

2. Blend on high for 2 minutes. Stir well and blend for a further minute.

3. Strain through a sieve into a jug. Pour into glasses filled with ice cubes.

SERVES 4

PREPARATION TIME 10 MINUTES

INGREDIENTS

4 large carrots, peeled and grated
500 ml / 18 fl. oz / 2 cups cold water
4 peaches, pitted, skinned and sliced
2 nectarines, pitted, skinned and sliced
1 lime, juiced
500 g / 1 lb 2 oz / 2 cups ice cubes

TOP TIP

Canned peaches or nectarines can be used if fresh ones are out of season.

Stress-free Smoothie

SERVES 4

PREPARATION TIME 10 MINUTES

INGREDIENTS

sticks of celery, peeled and chopped
avocados, peeled, pitted and diced
large cucumber, diced
lime, juiced
small handful of mint leaves
50 ml / 9 fl. oz / 1 cup almond milk
25 g / 8 oz / 1 cup plain yogurt
pinch of salt
0 g / 4 oz / ½ cup crushed ice

METHOD

1. Combine the celery, avocado, cucumber, lime juice and most of the mint leaves with the milk, plain yogurt and a pinch of salt in a food processor or blender.

2. Blend on high for 2 minutes, stirring halfway through, then add the crushed ice.

3. Stir well and blend for a further minute until smooth.

4. Pour into glasses and serve with a garnish of mint.

TOP TIP

Replace the almond milk with soy or coconut milk for a different taste.

Orange Pick-me-up

SERVES 4

PREPARATION TIME **10 MINUTES**

INGREDIENTS

4 large carrots, peeled and grated
4 Valencia oranges, juiced
1 lemon, juiced
5 cm (2 in) piece of root ginger, peeled and grated
250 ml / 9 fl. oz / 1 cup cold water
225 g / 8 oz / 1 cup crushed ice

METHOD

1. Combine the grated carrot, orange juice, lemon juice, ginger and water in a food processor or blender.

2. Blend on high for 2 minutes.

3. Add the crushed ice and blend for a further minute.

4. Pour into glasses and serve.

TOP TIP
Use 300 ml / 10 ½ fl. oz / 1 ½ cups orange juice (not from concentrate) in a pinch.

Grapefruit Refresher

SERVES 4

PREPARATION TIME 15 MINUTES

INGREDIENTS

2 pink grapefruit, peeled and segmented
2 white grapefruit, peeled and segmented
1 lime, juiced
225 g / 8 oz / 1 ½ cups white seedless grapes
250 ml / 9 fl. oz / 1 cup water
300 g / 10 ½ oz / 1 ⅓ cups crushed ice

METHOD

1. Combine the grapefruit segments with the lime juice, grapes and water in a food processor or blender.

2. Blend on high for a minute. Add the crushed ice and blend again for a further minute.

3. Pour into glasses and serve immediately for best results.

TOP TIP

Add 1–2 tbsp of agave nectar when blending to sweeten the juice.

Cranberry Tonic

SERVES 4

PREPARATION TIME 5 MINUTES

COOKING TIME 15 MINUTES

INGREDIENTS

2 limes
75 g / 3 oz / 1/3 cup caster (superfine) sugar
110 ml / 4 fl. oz / 1/2 cup water
1 l / 1 pint 16 fl. oz / 4 cups cranberry juice
500 ml / 18 fl. oz / 2 cups cold mineral water
500 g / 1 lb 2 oz / 2 cups ice cubes

METHOD

1. Juice one of the limes into a saucepan. Cut the other into wedges.

2. Add the sugar and water to the lime juice. Cook over a low heat, stirring, until the sugar has dissolved into a syrup. Allow to cool.

3. Combine with the cranberry juice in a pitcher. Add the water and ice cubes, stirring until chilled.

4. Pour into glasses and garnish with lime wedges.

TOP TIP
Try this tonic with sparkling water instead of still.

Berry Healer

METHOD

1. Set aside four cherries, strawberries, blueberries and raspberries.

2. Combine the remaining fruit with the water, ice, orange juice and icing sugar in a food processor or blender.

3. Blend on high for 2 minutes or until smooth.

4. Pour into glasses and garnish with the reserved fruit threaded onto skewers with a mint leaf. Dust with icing sugar before serving.

SERVES **4**

PREPARATION TIME **10 MINUTES**

INGREDIENTS

150 g / 5 oz / 1 cup cherries, pitted
150 g / 5 oz / 1 cup strawberries, hulled
125 g / 4 ½ oz / 1 cup blueberries
125 g / 4 ½ oz / 1 cup raspberries
75 g / 3 oz / ½ cup redcurrants
250 ml / 9 fl. oz / 1 cup cold water
225 g / 8 oz / 1 cup crushed ice
1 large orange, juiced
2 tbsp icing (confectioners') sugar, plus extra
    for dusting
a small handful of mint leaves

TOP TIP

Add a handful of baby kale or spinach before blending for an iron boost.

Citrus Kick

METHOD

1. Combine the lemon juice, water and agave nectar in a food processor or blender.

2. Blend on high for 1 minute until the agave has dissolved. Add the crushed ice and blend for another minute until frothy.

3. Pour into glasses and serve.

SERVES 4

PREPARATION TIME 10 MINUTES

INGREDIENTS

8 large lemons, juiced
1 l / 1 pint 16 fl. oz / 4 cups cold water
110 g / 4 oz / ½ cup light agave nectar
150 g / 5 oz / ²/₃ cup crushed ice

TOP TIP
Add a thumb-sized piece of grated ginger for its added digestive properties.

Energy Burst

METHOD

1. Combine all but four slices of the kiwi fruit with the pineapple and water in a food processor or blender.

2. Blend on high for 2 minutes.

3. Add the crushed ice and blend for a further minute.

4. Pour into glasses and garnish with a slice of kiwi on the rim and a sprinkling of flaked almonds on top.

SERVES 4

PREPARATION TIME 10 MINUTES

INGREDIENTS

6 kiwi fruit, peeled and sliced
½ small pineapple, peeled, cored and diced
250 ml / 9 fl. oz / 1 cup water
225 g / 8 oz / 1 cup crushed ice
1 tbsp flaked (slivered) almonds

TOP TIP
Substitute half the kiwi fruit for star fruit for a tropical accent.

Cleanse
and Detox

Watermelon and Strawberry Juice

SERVES **4**

PREPARATION TIME **15 MINUTES**

INGREDIENTS

300 g / 10 ½ oz / 2 cups strawberries, hulled
    and chopped
½ small watermelon, peeled, seeded and diced
250 ml / 9 fl. oz / 1 cup water
110 g / 4 oz / ½ cup crushed ice
4 sprigs of mint leaves, to garnish

METHOD

1. Mash the strawberries and watermelon wit
   a potato masher until broken down.

2. Combine the mashed fruit with the water
   and ice in a food processor or blender.
   Blend on high until smooth.

3. Pour into glasses and serve with a garnish
   of mint leaves.

TOP TIP
Add the juice of a lime
for a boost of
vitamin C.

Mango and Coconut Smoothie

SERVES 4

PREPARATION TIME 10 MINUTES

INGREDIENTS

1 coconut, split with water reserved
1 large mango, peeled, pitted and sliced
250 ml / 9 fl. oz / 1 cup light coconut milk
500 g / 1 lb 2 oz / 2 cups low-fat yogurt
2 tbsp light agave nectar

METHOD

1. Remove the flesh from the coconut and grate most of it into a food processor or blender, reserving some as a garnish. Add the reserved coconut water.

2. Add most of the mango, keeping aside four slices. Add the coconut milk, yogurt and agave nectar.

3. Blend on high for 2–3 minutes until smooth.

4. Pour into glasses and serve with a garnish of mango and coconut in the glass.

TOP TIP

Stir the mixture halfway through blending.

Kumquat and Pineapple Juice

SERVES 4

PREPARATION TIME 15 MINUTES

INGREDIENTS

1 small pineapple, peeled, cored and diced
300 g / 10 ½ oz / 2 cups kumquats, peeled
250 ml / 9 fl. oz / 1 cup orange juice
250 ml / 9 fl. oz / 1 cup cold sparkling water
1 lime, cut into wedges
55 g / 2 oz / ⅔ cup desiccated coconut

METHOD

1. Combine together the pineapple, kumquat flesh, orange juice and sparkling water in a food processor or blender.

2. Blend on high for 2 minutes until smooth. Rub the rims of four serving glasses with the lime wedges.

3. Dip the glasses in desiccated coconut to coat the rim. Fill with the juice before serving.

TOP TIP
Use chilled still water if sparkling is not available.

Exotic Punch with Berries

METHOD

1. Combine the mango juice, pineapple juice, lime juice and water in a food processor or blender.

2. Blend for 1 minute, add the crushed ice and blend for a further minute until frothy.

3. Pour into a pitcher and stir in the raspberries and mint leaves. Pour into glasses and serve.

SERVES 4

PREPARATION TIME 10 MINUTES

INGREDIENTS

500 ml / 18 fl. oz / 2 cups mango juice
500 ml / 18 fl. oz / 2 cups pineapple juice
2 limes, juiced
250 ml / 9 fl. oz / 1 cup cold sparkling water
225 g / 8 oz / 1 cup crushed ice
150 g / 5 oz / 1 cup raspberries
a small handful of mint leaves

TOP TIP
Blueberries or blackberries work well as a garnish in this drink.

Cucumber, Lettuce and Melon Medley

SERVES **4**

PREPARATION TIME **10 MINUTES**

INGREDIENTS

1 large cucumber
1 iceberg lettuce, shredded
½ small Honeydew melon, peeled, seeded
    and diced
4 nectarines, peeled, pitted and diced
250 ml / 9 fl. oz / 1 cup cold water

METHOD

1. Cut a few slices from the cucumber and reserve as a garnish. Chop the rest of the cucumber and place in a food processor or blender.

2. Add the lettuce, melon, nectarines and water.

3. Blend until smooth and serve in glasses garnished with the reserved cucumber.

TOP TIP

Add 150 g / 5 ¼ oz /
½ cup Greek yogurt
before blending for
added protein.

Pineapple, Lychee and Papaya Juice

SERVES 4

PREPARATION TIME 15 MINUTES

INGREDIENTS

300 g / 10 ½ oz / 2 cups lychees, peeled and pitted
½ small pineapple, peeled, cored and diced
1 papaya, peeled, seeded and diced
2 limes, juiced
250 ml / 9 fl. oz / 1 cup cold sparkling water
150 g / 5 oz / ²/₃ cup crushed ice

METHOD

1. Combine the fruit, lime juice and sparkling water in a food processor or blender.

2. Blend on high until smooth.

3. Add the crushed ice and blend for a further minute.

4. Pour into glasses and serve.

TOP TIP
Use 400 g / 14 oz / 2 ²/₃ cups of canned, drained lychees if fresh aren't available.

Pomegranate and Strawberry Juice

SERVES 4

PREPARATION TIME **10 MINUTES**

INGREDIENTS

450 g / 1 lb / 3 cups frozen strawberries
500 ml / 18 fl. oz / 2 cups water
1 pomegranate, halved

METHOD

1. Combine the strawberries and water in a food processor or blender.

2. Tap the back of the pomegranate halves with a wooden spoon to release their seeds. Add to the food processor or blender.

3. Blend on high until smooth and frothy.

4. Pour into glasses and serve.

TOP TIP
Add 225 g / 8 oz / ¾ cup of low-fat vanilla yogurt and blend to make a smoothie.

Lemon and Ginger Juice

SERVES **4**

PREPARATION TIME **10 MINUTES**

INGREDIENTS

1 l / 1 pint 16 fl. oz / 4 cups cold water
4 lemons, juiced
5 cm (2 in) piece of root ginger, peeled
110 g / 4 oz / ½ cup light agave nectar
500 g / 1 lb 2 oz / 2 cups ice cubes
a few sprigs of mint, to garnish

METHOD

1. Combine the water, lemon juice, ginger and agave nectar in a food processor or blender.

2. Blend until the agave has dissolved.

3. Fill glasses with ice cubes and pour over the lemon and ginger juice.

4. Garnish with mint sprigs before serving.

TOP TIP

Add a pinch of ground cinnamon to the juice for some extra warming spice.

Lime Juice

METHOD

1. Combine the lime juice, lemon juice, cucumber, sugar and water in a food processor or blender.

2. Blend on high until smooth.

3. Add the crushed ice and blend again for a further minute until frothy.

4. Pour into glasses and serve.

SERVES 4

PREPARATION TIME 15 MINUTES

INGREDIENTS

8 limes, juiced
2 lemons, juiced
½ small cucumber, chopped
75 g / 3 oz / ⅓ cup caster (superfine) sugar
500 ml / 18 fl. oz / 2 cups water
110 g / 4 oz / ½ cup crushed ice

TOP TIP
Try this juice recipe with sparkling rather than still water.

Beetroot and Apple Juice

SERVES 4

PREPARATION TIME **10 MINUTES**

INGREDIENTS

450 g / 1 lb / 3 cups cooked beetroot in juice
500 ml / 18 fl. oz / 2 cups apple juice
500 g / 1 lb 2 oz / 2 cups ice cubes

METHOD

1. Combine the beetroot and their juice with the apple juice in a food processor or blender.

2. Blend on high until smooth. Strain into a pitcher filled with the ice cubes.

3. Stir well until chilled. Pour into glasses and serve.

TOP TIP
Use a rubber spatula or pastry scraper to help pass the juice through the sieve.

Apple, Spinach and Lettuce Smoothie

SERVES **4**

PREPARATION TIME **10 MINUTES**

INGREDIENTS

100 g / 3 ½ oz / 2 cups baby spinach, washed
100 g / 3 ½ oz / 2 cups lamb's lettuce, washed
750 ml / 1 pint 6 fl. oz / 3 cups apple juice
1 lime, juiced
225 g / 8 oz / 1 cup crushed ice
a small handful of mint or apple mint leaves

METHOD

1. Combine the spinach, lamb's lettuce, apple juice and lime juice in a food processor or blender.

2. Blend on high for 2 minutes.

3. Add the crushed ice and mint leaves and blend for another minute until frothy.

4. Pour into glasses and serve.

TOP TIP
Add 2 tbsp of agave nectar for a boost of sweetness if needed.

Artichoke and Raspberry Smoothie

SERVES 4

PREPARATION TIME 10 MINUTES

INGREDIENTS

400 g / 14 oz / 2 cups canned artichoke
    hearts, drained
300 g / 10 ½ oz / 2 cups raspberries
250 ml / 9 fl. oz / 1 cup semi-skimmed milk
75 g / 3 oz / ⅓ cup maple syrup
½ lemon, juiced
225 g / 8 oz / 1 cup crushed ice
a few sprigs of mint, to garnish

METHOD

1. Combine the artichoke hearts, raspberries, milk, maple syrup and lemon juice in a food processor or blender.

2. Blend on high for 2 minutes.

3. Add the crushed ice and blend for a further minute until frothy.

4. Pour into glasses and garnish with a sprig of mint.

TOP TIP
For a dairy-free version, replace the milk with almond milk.

Green Smoothie with Parsley

SERVES 4

PREPARATION TIME 10 MINUTES

INGREDIENTS

1 avocado, peeled, pitted and diced
1 large cucumber, peeled and diced
1 lime, juiced
250 ml / 9 fl. oz / 1 cup pressed apple juice
a small bunch of flat-leaf parsley, torn
225 g / 8 oz / 1 ½ cups plain yogurt
110 g / 4 oz / ½ cup crushed ice

METHOD

1. Combine the avocado, cucumber, lime juice, apple juice, most of the parsley and the yogurt in a food processor or blender.

2. Blend on high for 2 minutes.

3. Add the crushed ice and blend for a further minute.

4. Pour into glasses and garnish with the remaining parsley.

TOP TIP

Try using pineapple juice in place of apple for a tropical version.

Avocado, Cucumber and Lemon Smoothie

SERVES 4

PREPARATION TIME 10 MINUTES

INGREDIENTS

2 avocados, peeled, pitted and diced
2 small cucumbers, peeled and diced
2 lemons, juiced
500 ml / 18 fl. oz / 2 cups almond milk
225 g / 8 oz / 1 cup crushed ice
a small bunch of dill, torn

METHOD

1. Combine the avocado, cucumber, lemon juice and almond milk in a food processor or blender.

2. Blend on high until smooth.

3. Add the crushed ice and most of the dill, then blend again for a further minute.

4. Pour into glasses and garnish with the remaining dill before serving.

TOP TIP

Blend in a handful of baby spinach for a boost of iron.

Fennel Smoothie

SERVES 4

PREPARATION TIME 5 MINUTES

INGREDIENTS

6 large fennel bulbs, fronds removed
     and reserved
1 lime, juiced
500 ml / 18 fl. oz / 2 cups pineapple juice
110 g / 4 oz / ½ cup plain yogurt
500 g / 1 lb 2 oz / 2 cups ice cubes

METHOD

1. Pass the fennel bulbs through a vegetable juicer, collecting the juice.

2. Combine the fennel juice with the lime juice, pineapple juice and plain yogurt in a food processor or blender.

3. Blend on high until smooth and frothy.

4. Pour into ice-filled glasses and serve with a garnish of fennel fronds.

TOP TIP

Try this smoothie with apple juice and a hint of grated ginger instead of pineapple.

Tomato and Strawberry Juice

SERVES 4

PREPARATION TIME 10 MINUTES

INGREDIENTS

450 g / 1 lb / 3 cups vine tomatoes, cored
   and seeded
300 g / 10 ½ oz / 2 cups frozen strawberries,
   hulled
250 ml / 9 fl. oz / 1 cup water
1 lime, juiced
1 tbsp light agave nectar

METHOD

1. Combine the tomatoes with the strawberries, water, lime juice and agave nectar in a food processor or blender.

2. Blend on high for 2–3 minutes until smooth.

3. Pour into glasses and serve.

TOP TIP

Blend in a handful of chopped watermelon for a refreshing addition.

INDEX